*25 Days of Christmas Devotional*

R. Joseph Ritter, Jr.

www.anticipatingchrist.com

© 2011, R. Joseph Ritter, Jr.

ISBN 978-1467952637


Author of *Sacrifice and Submission
In Marriage*




Scripture quotations taken from the
New American Standard Bible®,
Copyright © 1960, 1962, 1963, 1968, 1971, 1972, 1973,
1975, 1977, 1995 by The Lockman Foundation
Used by permission. (www.Lockman.org)


Cover Image Copyright Agata Dorobek, 2011.
Used under license from Shutterstock.com

Table of Contents

Introduction
December 1st – Anticipation
December 2nd – Looking for Adam and Eve
December 3rd – Going Back by a Different Way
December 4th – Reacting to Culture
December 5th – Lawful vs. Expedient
December 6th – Individualism Loses Again
December 7th – The Offensive Cross
December 8th – Taking Christ out of Christmas
December 9th – Decorating The Heart and Home
December 10th – The Colors of Christmas
December 11th – A Witness Through the Ages
December 12th – Beyond Rituals and Decorations
December 13th – The Christmas Tree
December 14th – Decorative Lights at Christmas
December 15th – Hungry for Food, Starving for the Gospel
December 16th – A Message for the Broken Hearted
December 17th – Angels Unaware
December 18th – Slowing Down
December 19th – Materialism
December 20th – The Smallest Gift
December 21st – Thriving in the Harsh Winter
December 22nd – A Lesson from St. Nicholas Santa Claus
December 23rd – Watching for Him
December 24th – Reflections on Christmas Eve
December 25th – Christmas Day

## Introduction

Christmas has always been my favorite season of the year. I can remember as a child anticipating Christmas while it was still summer time and looking through toy catalogs (we did not have a television growing up) to see what I might want to put on my wish list that year. Christmas is a time of anticipation, a time of celebration, a time of hope, and a time of love. It brings out the best in humanity. And now that I have children of my own, I look forward to the delight in their eyes and voices on Christmas Day.

When I married my wife, I was introduced to a different way of celebrating Christmas, and some of the differences caused me to launch a year-long inquiry into the history and origin of the Christmas traditions I have come to know and enjoy. In reading the historical accounts, stories and legends about our past and the many different traditions, I was continually struck by the work of God's hand in nature and through seasons. I am also intrigued by the response of people, both of long ago and of today, who knew deep within themselves that there was something more to life, something which caused events to occur, and something which required deep respect and much celebration.

Quite accidentally I found myself relating many of the historical accounts and origins of the traditions to Jesus Christ and was so moved at just how much Christ is (or can be, if we choose to see it) evident and alive through nature that I started to pen short devotionals. Out of this came a feeling of being led and inspired to write devotionals for the 25 days of Christmas, and it is my hope and prayer that God will work through this book in your heart and life.

# Anticipation

Scripture lesson for December 1st:

Job 19:25-27 "As for me, I know that my Redeemer lives, And at the last He will take His stand on the earth. 26 "Even after my skin is destroyed, Yet from my flesh I shall see God; 27 Whom I myself shall behold, And whom my eyes will see and not another. My heart faints within me!

~~~~~~~~~~~~~~~~~~~~~~~~~~~~~~~

Christmas is the season of advent. Wikipedia.org describes advent as "a time of expectant waiting and preparation for the celebration of the Nativity of Jesus at Christmas."

One of my favorite things to do as a child, especially on Christmas Eve, and I am sure I was not alone, was to sit in the living room and stare at the tree all lit up and decorated with presents underneath, wondering, hoping, anticipating. Children who believe in Santa Claus I am sure also sit and stare in longing expectation of Christmas morning. As I read through the Old Testament of the Bible, I am left with the same feelings of anticipation, hope and wonder. Unlike the Christ-child, my anticipations were fulfilled on the same day each year – December 25th. The readers of Old Testament prophecy, and most certainly the prophets themselves, had no idea of when their anticipation may be fulfilled.

Still, the hope and wonder of what was promised was enough to keep their eyes lifted heaven-ward, fixated on the Lord and anticipating the great day when their prophecies would be fulfilled. I am concerned that today's followers of Christ have lost a sense of anticipation – not for Christ's birth but for His *second coming*. Read the Scripture lesson again. Do you feel and truly believe Job's words and adopt them for yourself? Is this your desire?

As a child, I can remember singing the hymn in church *Work for the Night is Coming* when all work will be done. Despite the celebration at Christmas-time of Christ's birth, you still have something to anticipate – the Second Coming of our Lord and Savior Jesus Christ! The wikipedia.org entry for advent continues with this entry:

Latin adventus is the translation of the Greek word parousia, commonly used in reference to the Second Coming of Christ. For Christians, the season of Advent serves as a reminder both of the original waiting that was done by the Hebrews for the birth of their Messiah as well as the *waiting of Christians for Christ's return.* (Emphasis mine.)

Just like the Old Testament prophecies of His birth and reign, Jesus Himself promised in the New Testament that He would come again. But are you anticipating it? Are you longing with hope for that day? Are you working toward that day, readying yourself **and** those around you? Do you wonder with expectation what that day will be like?

Or have you allowed the cares of this world to get in the way and distract your attention?

Today, spend some time in prayer asking the Lord to renew your sense of anticipation of His second coming.

## Looking for Adam and Eve

Scripture lesson for December 2nd:

Genesis 3:6-11 When the woman saw that the tree was good for food, and that it was a delight to the eyes, and that the tree was desirable to make one wise, she took from its fruit and ate; and she gave also to her husband with her, and he ate. 7 Then the eyes of both of them were opened, and they knew that they were naked; and they sewed fig leaves together and made themselves loin coverings. 8 They heard the sound of the LORD God walking in the garden in the cool of the day, and the man and his wife hid themselves from the presence of the LORD God among the trees of the garden. 9 Then the LORD God called to the man, and said to him, "Where are you?" 10 He said, "I heard the sound of You in the garden, and I was afraid because I was naked; so I hid myself." 11 And He said, "Who told you that you were naked? Have you eaten from the tree of which I commanded you not to eat?"

~~~~~~~~~~~~~~~~~~~~~~~~~~~~~~

The factor which distinguishes the Christian faith from all other religions of the world is that the Lord actively seeks and pursues humanity. This has several important implications. The first is that the Lord is very much alive! He is not a piece of stone or wood and is not a distant star or galaxy. The second is that the Lord is very interested in you and very interested in what happens in your daily life. The third is that the Lord has the capacity to feel joy or heartache over the actions of humanity. And finally, the Lord has standards that He expects you to measure yourself against. It naturally follows, then, that there are consequences for failing to order your life to meet those standards, and that there are rewards for making the effort He expects. And this is why His coming is to be anticipated – to finally vindicate the wrongs in the world and to fulfill all of His promises to His followers. His coming is anticipated throughout the Bible, as is clearly stated in this Scripture:

> Isaiah 9:6-7 For a child will be born to us, a son will be given to us; And the government will rest on His shoulders; And His name will be called Wonderful Counselor, Mighty God, Eternal Father, Prince of Peace. 7 There will be no end to the increase of His government

or of peace, On the throne of David and over his kingdom, To establish it and to uphold it with justice and righteousness From then on and forevermore. The zeal of the LORD of hosts will accomplish this.

This Old Testament description written in anticipation of the coming Messiah confirms that the Lord seeks and pursues you. More than this, He promises you leadership and salvation. And He is with you. Isaiah 7:14 and Matthew 1:23 both foretell that the Messiah will be called Immanuel, which means "God with us." A God who desires to be with you, who seeks to have a relationship with you, and who pursues you with His salvation is a God who is worth knowing!

No matter how far into the depths of despair you may travel; no matter what lengths you go to put distance between you and the Lord; no matter how difficult your circumstances or how difficult your suffering; no matter the sins or crimes you may have committed, the Lord who pursued Adam and Eve after their cosmic rebellion actively seeks and pursues you and desires to have a relationship with you. Although the Lord will hold you to account for your behavior and let you feel the consequences of your decisions, He does not wait for an opportunity to hit you over the head with a club. Instead, He waits with love and forgiveness – but it is up to you to make the first step, to accept His salvation and to surrender to His pursuit of you. Let Him find you today.

Today, take some time to reflect on the Lord's pursuit of you. Then, stop running from Him long enough for you to find Him.

## Going Back By a Different Way

Scripture lesson for December 3rd:

Matt 2:1-12 Now after Jesus was born in Bethlehem of Judea in the days of Herod the king, magi from the east arrived in Jerusalem, saying, 2 "Where is He who has been born King of the Jews? For we saw His star in the east and have come to worship Him." 3 When Herod the king heard this, he was troubled, and all Jerusalem with him. 4 Gathering together all the chief priests and scribes of the people, he inquired of them where the Messiah was to be born. 5 They said to him, "In Bethlehem of Judea; for this is what has been written by the prophet: 6 'AND YOU, BETHLEHEM, LAND OF JUDAH, ARE BY NO MEANS LEAST AMONG THE LEADERS OF JUDAH; FOR OUT OF YOU SHALL COME FORTH A RULER WHO WILL SHEPHERD MY PEOPLE ISRAEL.'" 7 Then Herod secretly called the magi and determined from them the exact time the star appeared. 8 And he sent them to Bethlehem and said, "Go and search carefully for the Child; and when you have found Him, report to me, so that I too may come and worship Him." 9 After hearing the king, they went their way; and the star, which they had seen in the east, went on before them until it came and stood over the place where the Child was. 10 When they saw the star, they rejoiced exceedingly with great joy. 11 After coming into the house they saw the Child with Mary His mother; and they fell to the ground and worshiped Him. Then, opening their treasures, they presented to Him gifts of gold, frankincense, and myrrh. 12 And having been warned by God in a dream not to return to Herod, the magi left for their own country by another way.

~~~~~~~~~~~~~~~~~~~~~~~~~~~~~~~

In today's Scripture lesson, it seems quite obvious why the wise men went back by another way after having an encounter with Jesus – they were warned in a dream.

But there is more to the story than a simple dream. To get to Jesus, they followed the pathway of evil by going directly to King Herod. King Herod wanted to kill Jesus. This is already starting to sound very familiar, isn't it? You and I followed the pathway of evil before encountering Jesus Christ, and Satan has been working feverishly for thousands of years to destroy Jesus. Do you see the similarities? Yet let's continue.

In their encounter with Jesus, the wise men brought expensive gifts, they worshiped Jesus, and they rejoiced at having found Him and because He was born. Think back to your first encounter with Jesus. Take a moment to remember what it was like. A lot of people describe it as a great day, a day when a heavy burden was lifted or when they had such extreme joy. In the weeks, months and years since that first encounter, you have no doubt worshiped Jesus Christ in church, in prayer and in other ways. You have also no doubt given sacrificially of yourself with your time, skill, your effort, and even your financial and other tangible resources.

Now consider that, if the wise men had gone back by the same way they came to Jesus, they would have walked right into Satan's snare. If the way by which you traveled to get to Jesus is filled with heartache, pain, regret, guilt and shame, why would you want to go back that same road? Why would you want to walk right back into Satan's snare?

Going back by a different way, then, is the beginning of the process of transformation. It is an acknowledgment that the road you traveled to get to Jesus is not the same road which is to be traveled again if you are to enter into a meaningful relationship with Jesus. It is an admission of sins in your life up until the day of your encounter with Jesus Christ.

No one can have a meaningful encounter with Jesus and go back the same way they came.

But going back by a different way is not easy. It is an unknown. Even though it is the road which leads to a life with Jesus Christ, it is a road you have never traveled before. The destination is unknown. The experiences you will encounter along the way are unknown. But placing your trust in Christ is a significant part of the transformation process. Christ knows where the road leads. He knows the experiences you will face. He understands the uncertainty. Take comfort in knowing that there is no experience Christ has not already encountered, no uncertainty He has not already faced, and no road He has not already traveled. Keeping Christ as your guide, you will not get lost or sink in the despair of difficult experiences or be left alone in insurmountable circumstances.

This is the challenge presented by Christ. Will you go back a different way? There is a way which leads to life, and Christ stands ready to be your guide along that way. Won't you step out in faith and trust Christ to lead you a different way?

Today, ask the Lord to light your path and to show you which road you are traveling. If you have already encountered Jesus, but you are on the same road you used to get to Him, ask the Lord to show you how to go by a different way.

## Reacting to Culture

Scripture lesson for December 4th:

Ezra 7:10 For Ezra had set his heart to study the law of the LORD and to practice it, and to teach His statutes and ordinances in Israel. Ezra 9:3 When I heard about this matter, I tore my garment and my robe, and pulled some of the hair from my head and my beard, and sat down appalled.

~~~~~~~~~~~~~~~~~~~~~~~~~~~~~~

Today and for the next two days, I have inserted thoughts from an unpublished compilation I titled *Tales from the Back Pew*. Although they were not originally meant for the Christmas season, they are intended to provoke your thinking.

It is no coincidence that the text in 9:3 comes *after* 7:10. Ezra here highlights that his reaction in 9:3 to the sins of Israel is a product of his commitment and beliefs expressed in 7:10. There is a note in the margin of my Bible at 9:3 which I handwrote at some point – "Do we react like this today?"

Or have today's followers of Christ become desensitized to sin – this desensitization being a byproduct of the media, news, television, movies, Internet, politicians, video games, etc. or perhaps even the general condition of the Christian church and the attack on general Protestant beliefs. Few today are (really) not appalled at the sins of American culture or even of the members of the church down the street because they are no longer appalled at reports of sins in the fictional world of television and novels or the level of corruption in government. It is as if they have come to expect it, as if the outward showing of sins in the lives of people is the norm.

But Ezra makes no mention of becoming desensitized to sins in Israel's culture more than two thousand years ago. The one place in the Bible this type of atmosphere is discussed is Genesis 6:5-8, 11-13, where it says:

> Then the LORD saw that the wickedness of man was great on the earth, and that every intent of the thoughts of his heart was only

> evil continually. 6 The LORD was sorry that He had made man on the earth, and He was grieved in His heart. 7 The LORD said, "I will blot out man whom I have created from the face of the land, from man to animals to creeping things and to birds of the sky; for I am sorry that I have made them." 8 But Noah found favor in the eyes of the LORD. 11 Now the earth was corrupt in the sight of God, and the earth was filled with violence. 12 God looked on the earth, and behold, it was corrupt; for all flesh had corrupted their way upon the earth. 13 Then God said to Noah, "The end of all flesh has come before Me; for the earth is filled with violence because of them; and behold, I am about to destroy them with the earth.

Just how bad were they? Is it possible they were more sinful than American culture in the 21st century?

The image brought to mind in Genesis 6 is that the whole culture was infiltrated by sin, even infiltrating the very imaginations of the mind. This sounds like 21st century American culture – political corruption, news media reports of various and sundry crimes and social problems, Hollywood's television and film productions more often than not portray violence, glorify social problems (single-parent families, divorce, child violence, criminal activity, deviant behavior, teen pregnancy, infidelity, homosexuality, etc.), personal failures even in the church, and so on.

You are bombarded every moment of every day by information, and the majority of that information contains references to problems in society and the propensity to do evil or influence the cause of an evil act.

But Ezra does not mention any of this desensitization. Instead, you can plainly see that Ezra's reaction to the sins of Israel is directly attributable to his study of the Scriptures. Would you react differently if you made it a point to have a firm understanding of the Scriptures which were divinely inspired by the Lord?

Do you want to possess such understanding and belief? That is a question each individual must deal with, and I trust you do want to possess that understanding and belief. Seeking these things is the only way to produce real change and have a real impact on American culture. This is the message Ezra has for 21st century America and it still rings true today.

The real question, however, is not how you react but what are you going to do based upon your reactions? To put it another way, you (and I) should be challenged to pray for our culture and our political and church leaders. The Lord still hears and answers prayer, but the Lord also still only moves primarily through the Holy Spirit. It is when you are filled with the Holy Spirit that you are moved to act and react in the ways described by Ezra.

If nothing else, let this lesson influence the gifts you give your family this Christmas season. But my prayer is that you will let the eyes of your heart be open to where the culture is and where the Lord wants you to be.

Today, make a list of the television shows you watch, the video games you play (or let your children play), and the books and magazines you read. Then ask yourself this question: Would I do these same things or even display them if Jesus came *in the flesh* to my home today?

## *Lawful vs. Expedient*

Scripture lesson for December 5th:

I Corinthians 10:23-24 All things are lawful, but not all things are profitable. All things are lawful, but not all things edify. 24 Let no one seek his own good, but that of his neighbor.

~~~~~~~~~~~~~~~~~~~~~~~~~~~~~~~

Another way of looking at the title for today is "My Rights vs. What is Advantageous for Me." I have the right to smoke a cigarette just as much as my neighbor has the right to clean air. I have the right to live a promiscuous (homosexual, pre-marital sex, extra-marital affair, pornography) lifestyle just as much as the virgin has the right to live in abstinence until marriage. I have the right to tailgate the car in front of me at 80 MPH just as much as the driver following me has the right to keep a distance of five car-lengths.

But that's not the issue. What you are entitled to or what is the most fun today is not important. Instead, you (and I) must look through the lens of "advantageousness." That's a big word, so let's unpack it a little.

All things are lawful for me... well, maybe except for those things that could land me in jail. Ok, how about an easy one; you're driving down the interstate at 80 MPH, and the guy in front of you is going 75. You tailgate the other driver to send a message that they should move out of the way. Whether your driving deserves a ticket for tailgating/speeding isn't the question; we're not talking about getting caught, we're only examining the wisdom behind the decision. So the driver eventually moves out of the way, and you speed on. Right? Not this time. A tire on the tractor trailer up ahead blows out; your view is blocked by the driver your following and you don't see the huge chunks of rubber in the road, when WHAM! your car hits the biggest chunk of rubber.

Was it an advantageous decision to tailgate? Probably not, especially considering your car is now damaged.

This is the message Paul has for you in the 21st century American culture. Not necessarily everything you could possibly do, see or enjoy in this life is advantageous for you. Not everything is expedient, although just about everything might be lawful.

It's the same way with the Lord. Paul says to let all things be done unto edifying. *Thayer's Lexicon* defines edify to mean architecture. You should only concern yourself with those things that are expedient and those things that edify. What things are expedient? What things edify? Who or what is being edified? For an answer, let's look together at Matthew 16:13-18:

> Now when Jesus came into the district of Caesarea Philippi, He was asking His disciples, "Who do people say that the Son of Man is?" 14 And they said, "Some say John the Baptist; and others, Elijah; but still others, Jeremiah, or one of the prophets." 15 He [!] said to them, "But who do you say that I am?" 16 Simon Peter answered, "You are the Christ, the Son of the living God." 17 And Jesus said to him, "Blessed are you, Simon Barjona, because flesh and blood did not reveal this to you, but My Father who is in heaven. 18 "I also say to you that you are Peter, and upon this rock I will build My church; and the gates of Hades will not overpower it.

The things that are expedient are those that will be most helpful to your belief that Jesus Christ is the Son of the living God. The things you do should construct and build up in yourself, your family, and your congregation the belief that Jesus is the Christ, the Son of the Living God. I like the definition of edifying as architecture. The gospel of Christ is (or should be) the architecture by which everything is constructed... including Christmas.

Today, take a few minutes to think about your most common habits. Then list them in columns, one column for habits that edify Christ and the other for those things which may be disadvantageous. Take the rest of this Christmas season to pray over the list.

## Individualism Loses Again

Scripture lesson for December 6th:

Jeremiah 29:4-7, 11 "Thus says the LORD of hosts, the God of Israel, to all the exiles whom I have sent into exile from Jerusalem to Babylon, 5 'Build houses and live in them; and plant gardens and eat their produce. 6 'Take wives and become the fathers of sons and daughters, and take wives for your sons and give your daughters to husbands, that they may bear sons and daughters; and multiply there and do not decrease. 7 'Seek the welfare of the city where I have sent you into exile, and pray to the LORD on its behalf; for in its welfare you will have welfare.' 11 'For I know the plans that I have for you,' declares the LORD, 'plans for welfare and not for calamity to give you a future and a hope. See also I Kings 2:2-4.

~~~~~~~~~~~~~~~~~~~~~~~~~~~~~~

Nobody likes to be under the thumb of another person. Children test the bounds of parents' authority; peasants revolt against the monarch; and the employee tries to rise up in the ranks of management. Through Jeremiah, however, the Lord reveals to the world that it is not your place to seek only your own welfare.

Another way of looking at this is to say that it is the wrong decision to wiggle out of the grip of authority rather than to be content and promote the welfare of everyone. Parents teach their kids valuable lessons every day – you have to take the good with the bad, or sometimes you have to do things you don't like to do in order to function in society. The Lord is telling you that, before He can prosper you, you must prosper those around you. It may sound counter-intuitive, but let's continue.

This has all the makings of a true servant. Christ Himself chose to prosper all of us by dying on the cross. He left the glory of heaven where He sat at the right hand of God the Father, so that He could be crucified on the cross for your sins and make it possible for you and me to be made right with Him and live in community with Him. Having overcome death, He returned to heaven to again sit at the right hand of God the Father. He could have stayed in heaven and never come to earth, but He put you first.

As was discussed a few days ago, you are bombarded with information in every moment of every day. Your life may be busy, hectic and pulling at you in every direction. So when you stumble across someone in need, it's all too easy to keep going in the name of "life." But is that what life is all about? I, for one, certainly hope not, and I urge you to allow your heart to be examined, so that you can see in what areas of your life the Lord wants changes to be made.

Consider the following real-life encounters followers of Christ had and what the outcome was:

> Some people from the church took groceries to a needy family; twelve years later, a child from that family is in theological seminary preparing for the ministry.
>
> A family joined together in prayer for another family member who had dropped out of church to pursue alcohol and the fast life; five years later, that family member is back in church and on solid ground again.
>
> A divorced woman who lived alone down the road was lonely, depressed and having difficulty with her adult children; a minister and his family befriend her and nearly twenty years later, she was singing church hymns and full of joy in the midst of extreme pain as a friend drove her to the hospital where she later died, sure of her place in heaven.
>
> A young family struggles to make ends meet; a group of men from the local church help them fix up their house to make it a better place for the family to live in; the young children in that family are turned into givers.

What were the immediate benefits that the "servants" in these (true) stories received? Actually, there were none; in each of these stories, it "cost" the servants something – time, money, resources. It was time, money and resources they could have spent somewhere else. The results are not always immediate, but there will be results. Sometimes you (the servant) may never see the result. But God the Father promises blessings untold in heaven.

It's a little thing the Bible refers to as obedience. You cannot obey anybody when all you do is look for instant gratification. If they don't get some kind of pleasure out of something right now, most people quit. Being a servant requires experiencing an instant *cost* – not instant *gain*!

Did you ever get something for free? Did you ever stop to think that it cost someone somewhere something, so that you could get that free item? Retail stores use this tactic on a regular basis – the result they hope for is branding, which is another way of saying "repeat customer." For the retailer, it's an investment in the future. The sacrifices you make today are an investment in *your* future.

Being content with what you have, helping others out and seeking to improve the welfare of those around you are some of the marks of a Christian lifestyle. The problem is, most people don't follow this kind of lifestyle because it costs too much today. The Lord promises that you will have a reward – He assures you of either a reward here on earth or a reward in heaven. If you choose to have the reward now, you are certain to lose out on an eternal, heavenly reward. If you choose to have the reward later, it will cost you now, but it's a reward that will be most satisfying.

Nothing's free! Pay now or pay later, but someday you'll pay. If you ask me, I'd rather pay as a servant and have the reward of a king later. But that's just me.

Today, take some time to prayerfully consider whom you may have an encounter with this Christmas season and what you can do to make a radical impact on their lives. Let me make a few suggestions: 1) Give the waitress at your favorite restaurant a large tip (maybe $50 or $100); 2) give a grocery store gift card or gas card to a family without a steady source of income; or 3) when you see someone in your neighborhood moving in or out, go help them – chances are they are going through financial difficulties or a job change and those things are hard enough without having to also make the adjustment of moving at Christmas.

## The Offensive Cross

Scripture lesson for December 7th:

Gal 5:6-13 For in Christ Jesus neither circumcision nor uncircumcision means anything, but faith working through love. 7 You were running well; who hindered you from obeying the truth? 8 This persuasion did not come from Him who calls you. 9 A little leaven leavens the whole lump of dough. 10 I have confidence in you in the Lord that you will adopt no other view; but the one who is disturbing you will bear his judgment, whoever he is. 11 But I, brethren, if I still preach circumcision, why am I still persecuted? Then the stumbling block of the cross has been abolished. 12 I wish that those who are troubling you would even mutilate themselves. 13 For you were called to freedom, brethren; only do not turn your freedom into an opportunity for the flesh, but through love serve one another.

~~~~~~~~~~~~~~~~~~~~~~~~~~~~~~

This year, as in so many years before, some people will cut down a real Christmas tree and bring it into their homes. Others will get a real tree from a lot. Still others, like myself, will unpack a tree from a box. But just what does the Christmas tree represent?

Some people refer to Jesus Christ dying on a tree. The original purpose of bringing an evergreen tree into the home hundreds of years ago in Europe was to capture the mysterious powers of the tree that enabled it to stay green during the harsh winter and to warm the home with life while the world outside was cold and dark.

Because even hundreds of years ago the Christmas tree represented everlasting life and today it can be used as a teaching lesson about Jesus Christ dying on the cross, it should be no wonder why Christmas and the tree are offensive to so many.

Christmas represents the anticipation of the coming of Christ. But just what does the cross represent? One of the best depictions of the cross I have seen is in the *Fireproof* movie. In this particular scene, the lead actor, Caleb, is walking with his father in a remote campground. In the center of the campground is a cross. As the two are walking toward the center of the campground, they discuss Caleb's marriage, and his father introduces him to Christ. Caleb's father asks him what frustrates him the most about his wife. Caleb begins to express his frustration. While going on and on about how bad his wife and his marriage are, Caleb sits down in the shadow of the cross with his head to the ground. At the conclusion of his outburst, he asks, "How am I supposed to show love to someone over and over and over who constantly rejects me?" As he is talking, his father walks to the cross and leans on it. Caleb finally looks up, and his father says, "That's a good question." During a long pause, Caleb is confronted with the love of Christ and the offensive cross.

This is exactly who Jesus is – He loves you over and over and over despite being continually rejected by the very people He created and died for! Charles Spurgeon in his 1856 sermon *The Offense of the Cross*, updated and revised by Tony Capoccia (2000), says:

> gentle as the gospel is, and inoffensive as its professors have also proved themselves to be ... there has never been anything which has caused more disturbance in the world than the Christian religion. It is not a sword, and yet it has brought war into the world; it is not a fire, and yet it has consumed many old institutions, and has burned much that men thought would last forever; it is the gospel of peace, and yet it has separated the dearest of friends, and caused terrible feuds and confusions everywhere... What exactly is the offense of the cross? ... The philosopher looks at the cross and then says, 'I cannot see anything wonderful in it, even though I can see more clearly than the poor, humble peasant...' The man who loves controversy comes to the gospel, and ... says ..., 'I will not listen to your preacher who says, 'This is the truth, the whole truth, and nothing but the truth.' I will not listen to the man who speaks to authoritatively; I like men who will give me enough room to doubt, who let me believe what I like; I prefer to use my reason and common sense...' The man who is relying on his own strength for salvation, does not like the doctrine of the cross. If anyone preaches a gospel which ... starts to cast the sinner down in the dust and to teach what Christ himself taught, 'No one can come to me unless the Father who sent me draws him;' and that, in the Scriptures, all men are declared to be 'dead in transgressions and sins;' then the proud sinner will turn away, and says, 'I am not going to be so insulted, as to have all my powers leveled to the ground!' ... And again the cross offends men and

women, because it is contrary to their ideas of human worth. There is not a soul in all the world that, by nature, loves to be stripped of all worth. No! the last thing a man likes to part with is his righteousness... But there is another offense, which is a very painful one, and the world has never yet forgiven the cross for that 'offense' – the offense that the cross will not recognize any distinctions between mankind.

Indeed, there is a gift waiting under the tree for everyone – a gift of love and grace. Although sin knows no boundaries, love and grace also know no boundaries. And for some reason that is offensive.

Today you have been confronted with the cross. Will you accept the Lord's love and grace?

## Taking Christ Out of Christmas

Scripture lesson for December 8th:

Luke 12:4-5 "I say to you, My friends, do not be afraid of those who kill the body and after that have no more that they can do. 5 "But I will warn you whom to fear: fear the One who, after He has killed, has authority to cast into hell; yes, I tell you, fear Him!

~~~~~~~~~~~~~~~~~~~~~~~~~~~~~~~

Somewhere along the line it has become objectionable to wish a stranger "Merry Christmas." Instead, we are led to believe that we should say, "Happy Holidays." I have heard many folks denounce such efforts as attempts to remove Christmas from Christmas. And no doubt like me you have seen bumper stickers that say, "Keep Christ in Christmas."

It is unfortunate that today's secular culture has taken such a neutral and even adversarial position toward Christmas. Some people are actually concerned that a greeting of "Merry Christmas" will be offensive to a few people, and *there are a few people* who have become offended by the sights, symbols and sounds of Christmas. After yesterday, it should be no wonder that some want to take Christ out of Christmas. I know some people who say they do not believe in Christmas. They know very well what Christmas represents – Jesus Christ – and they want nothing to do with Him.

It should be no surprise, then, that the culture is trying to do away with Christ and His symbolism. In today's world, persecution occurs in essentially every part of the world – including North America. In times past, many missionaries and followers of Christ have endured horrific persecution and have even been killed for their beliefs and for refusing to renounce Christ. Accounts of some who have been killed for their faith and what they taught appear as early as in the New Testament of the Bible.

Despite such difficulties, it is not uncommon to hear stories of followers of Christ who had nothing else to rely on but memorized verses and passages of the Bible. And they prayed. They also remembered the times of fellowship and worship they once enjoyed. No matter what hardships come your way, no one can strip away the things which have been etched on your heart and mind.

It reminds me of the little boy who for his punishment was told to sit in a chair in the corner. He complied but defiantly said, "I may be sitting down on the outside, but I am standing up on the inside!" People and the culture may influence or even dictate how you outwardly conduct yourself. But nothing can take away what you have allowed to be etched on your heart and mind. The culture may persecute the followers of Christ, and the government may outlaw the practice of assembling together for worship and may even outlaw and destroy all Bibles. But nothing can stop the followers of Christ from praying and nothing can stop them from reciting memorized Scriptures.

This raises some interesting questions, including what you would have to cling to if you were imprisoned for your faith. But it also presents a very unique opportunity to get into a very deep and meaningful relationship with Christ and to place all hope and trust in Him.

So let the culture take Christmas out of Christmas. But they can't take away the memories, the excitement, the anticipation and the belief and faith you have. They also can't take away the reality of Christ and His triumphant second coming. All glory to God!

Today, take some time to thank the Lord for the freedoms you do have, and then ask Him to write His statutes on your heart.

## Decorating The Heart and Home

Scripture lesson for December 9th:

Revelation 3:19-22 'Those whom I love, I reprove and discipline; therefore be zealous and repent. 20 'Behold, I stand at the door and knock; if anyone hears My voice and opens the door, I will come in to him and will dine with him, and he with Me. 21 'He who overcomes, I will grant to him to sit down with Me on My throne, as I also overcame and sat down with My Father on His throne. 22 'He who has an ear, let him hear what the Spirit says to the churches.'"

~~~~~~~~~~~~~~~~~~~~~~~~~~~~~~

By now a few Christmas decorations have probably been hung in your home. Each Christmas, families everywhere prepare by putting up lights, colors of green and red, the tree by the window all decorated with ornaments, stockings dangling from the hearth, tinsel clinging to the railing of the stairwell, and beautifully wrapped gifts piled under the tree. Pretty soon the sights, sounds and smells of family will fill the air – the ham or turkey in the oven, the music and laughter, and aunts and uncles not seen in months or perhaps years. And children will be throwing paper off their presents and shouting in excitement.

You may go to great lengths to heighten the joy of the season, to make memories and to fill the home with love. But do you prepare your heart in the same way for the coming of Jesus? Do you pull out your finest decorations for Him? Do you cook your best meals? Do you joyfully welcome Him in? Do you play your best music and bring out the finest china? Or does He only get what's left and served only with the everyday dishes and utensils? And is He given only a portion of your time?

Christ came into this world much the same way He was treated during His lifetime on earth – relegated to the stables and to sleep on the hay eaten by the animals. A hospital? A clean place to sleep? No! His parents were poor and had no health insurance! A motel room? A house? No! There was no room for Him, no one wanted to let Him in. He and his parents were strangers, they were outcasts, and no one wanted to be associated with them. The way He was born is the same way He died – an outcast.

He was arrested as a common criminal, beaten and whipped as a thief, and crucified as a murderer. Yet He broke no laws, healed the sick and the lame, He stole nothing from God in His divine equality, and gave you life by giving up His own. Is Christ treated any better than a common criminal today? The government says He is intrusive and intolerant, His name cannot be uttered on the ball field, His book cannot appear in schools, His cross cannot show up in a condominium, and His tree cannot be erected at city hall. He who has no equal is told to wait His turn at the military base chapel; He who was publicly humiliated for bringing you salvation is expected to stand by and watch the pride marches on Main Street; He who breathes life into all creation is coerced into standing behind the protestors' line while babies are aborted; He who triumphed over evil and conquered death is locked in a jail cell while war rages on; He who commands an army of angels is bound and gagged and told to watch while the blood of His believers is shed; and He who humbly lay in a manger on a bed of hay is given a citation to tear down His barn lest the homeless, orphans and hungry come to find shelter from a cruel world.

The Lord will not be mocked! It may seem to you and me that He is thrown into a box and legislated out of existence. But God's purposes will not be frustrated!

Jesus is coming, and that is why we celebrate! So tell me, how will you prepare for a visit by the Creator of the universe? The Savior of the World? You go to great lengths to prepare your home for guests at Christmas. You celebrate with your friends and family. But do you prepare for Christ? Do you celebrate with Him? Or do you even want to open the door to your heart for Him because you're afraid of what He might find?

Today, ask the Lord to show you if there are any areas of your heart that perhaps you have been hesitant to allow Him into, and then invite Him in.

## The Colors of Christmas

Scripture lesson for December 10th:

Isaiah 1:18 "Come now, and let us reason together," Says the LORD, "Though your sins are as scarlet, They will be as white as snow; Though they are red like crimson, They will be like wool.
Jeremiah 17:8 "For he will be like a tree planted by the water, That extends its roots by a stream And will not fear when the heat comes; But its leaves will be green, And it will not be anxious in a year of drought Nor cease to yield fruit.
Revelation 3:18 I advise you to buy from Me gold refined by fire so that you may become rich, and white garments so that you may clothe yourself, and that the shame of your nakedness will not be revealed; and eye salve to anoint your eyes so that you may see.

~~~~~~~~~~~~~~~~~~~~~~~~~~~~~~~

The popular colors which have come to symbolize Christmas are red, green, and gold. Ace Collins in the *Stories Behind the Great Traditions of Christmas* (Zondervan / 2003) writes that these "three colors were not just haphazardly splashed on the canvas of the season but were born out of existing holiday customs combined with the knowledge of Jesus' life."

He continues by saying that ancient civilizations were most fascinated by the red berries that came from holly plants in the middle of winter. The poinsettia is another interesting plant because its greenery blends in with all the other plants, until just before Christmas when the leaves turn scarlet. And the legend of St. Nicholas which has survived from the fourth century is that he wore a red robe. Red is associated with the blood of Christ, and it is mentioned 53 times in the Bible.

Green is the color of mystery and life, most notably for its connection to grass, trees and evergreens. Ace Collins goes on to write that early humankind did not comprehend what made evergreen plants live year round, but they knew the greenery was special and symbolized life. Green is, thus, associated with the birth and life of Jesus Christ, and it is mentioned 41 times in the Bible.

Ace Collins continues with gold which has the clearest association with the Christian faith. It was one of the gifts brought by the wise men, and it is the color associated with wealth and royalty. Certainly it seems appropriate that Jesus who would one day be mocked as King of the Jews would be associated with the color of the royal heads of state. For Christmas, gold has come to represent light, and light represents the illumination that Christ brought into the world. Gold is mentioned 417 times in the Bible.

Everywhere you look in the world you can see red, green, and gold. They are colors of nature, and it is no mistake that Jesus Christ would use nature to draw you to Himself, especially since He is the Creator!

Now let's look more closely at today's Scripture lesson. The blood of Jesus Christ washes away your sins. A green tree is the source of fruit. And Jesus Christ enables you to be wealthy beyond imagine. Now apply these colors and these verses to yourself. With the blood of Jesus Christ, you can be made to have a relationship with Him. With the life Jesus Christ gives, you can bear fruit in a world full of people who are hungry to know Jesus Christ. And seeking to root your life in Jesus Christ will give you His wealth in heaven, a far better reward than all the gold the world has to offer.

Today take a moment to soak in the colors of Christmas. As you look forward to the coming of the Christmas season, let the anticipation of the coming of Christ build in you. To prepare for that day, you can have forgiveness of your sins through Christ, you can have a ready answer for your faith before your family, friends and co-workers, and you can live a life which Jesus Christ will find pleasing.

## A Witness Through the Ages

Scripture lesson for December 11th:

Exodus 12:12-14 'For I will go through the land of Egypt on that night, and will strike down all the firstborn in the land of Egypt, both man and beast; and against all the gods of Egypt I will execute judgments—I am the LORD. 13 'The blood shall be a sign for you on the houses where you live; and when I see the blood I will pass over you, and no plague will befall you to destroy you when I strike the land of Egypt. 14 'Now this day will be a memorial to you, and you shall celebrate it as a feast to the LORD; throughout your generations you are to celebrate it as a permanent ordinance.

~~~~~~~~~~~~~~~~~~~~~~~~~~~~~~~

I was sitting in church a few Sundays before Thanksgiving, contemplating the final devotional thoughts for this book, and it was communion Sunday. As I watched the servers in the choir loft straining to deliver the communion elements in the tight quarters of the chancel area, I was struck with the image of a person sharing Christ.

Why communion? Jesus Christ fulfilled the Passover and extended all the benefits of the Passover to all people. The Scripture lesson today is a reminder of what occurred in the first Passover. The Lord was in the middle of pronouncing judgments in the form of plagues on Egypt. The Pharaoh of Egypt held the people of Israel, the Lord's chosen people, captive, and the Lord was trying to get Pharaoh's attention. Pharaoh's heart was hardened, however, and he never turned his face toward the Lord. One of the plagues was the death of every firstborn child, which was to be carried out by the angels of the Lord. The Lord promised that the angels would "pass over" the house of anyone who had the blood of a spotless lamb painted on their doorpost.

Jesus Christ took upon Himself the Passover. He became the blood of the Lamb. You (and I) now have the opportunity to paint our hearts with the blood of the lamb.

At Christmas, you (hopefully) anticipate the coming of Christ. You may anticipate His coming with joy, but there is a whole other segment of the world's population which either doesn't know or doesn't care that Christ is coming again. The Lord's wrath was poured out on Pharaoh, and it will be poured out again on the evil in the world. Like the Israelites in Egypt, you can be safe from the Lord's wrath by being washed in the blood of the lamb.

It is the greatest gift you can give another person – better than any present under the tree. Next time communion is served in your church, imagine that the servers are making it possible for the person receiving the juice, which represents the blood of Christ, to paint the doorpost of their heart with the blood of the lamb. Then imagine yourself taking the message of the gospel to a person who may otherwise receive the wrath of the Lord in the second coming of Christ.

Now, why would anyone want to anticipate wrath for Christmas? Or should I ask, who wants a lump of coal at Christmas?

Today, prayerfully consider who in your circle of influence may be in need of the gospel message of Christ. Then ask the Lord to use you as a witness to those people.

## Beyond Rituals and Decorations

Scripture lesson for December 12th:

Psalm 51:16-17 For You do not delight in sacrifice, otherwise I would give it; You are not pleased with burnt offering. 17 The sacrifices of God are a broken spirit; A broken and a contrite heart, O God, You will not despise.

~~~~~~~~~~~~~~~~~~~~~~~~~~~~~~

Back in Leviticus, the Lord gave His people a set of laws to live by. Breaking those laws resulted in sin, and sin could only be atoned by making a sacrifice of a lamb. The Lord also prescribed a number of different offerings. The people regularly made sacrifices and also made many offerings. In fact, the story of Cain and Abel in Genesis centers around making an offering to the Lord.

With this system of sacrifices and offerings in the background, it seems hard to understand why the Psalmist writes that the Lord does not delight in sacrifice and is not pleased with a burnt offering. Jesus provides the explanation in Matthew 12:28-33:

> One of the scribes came and heard them arguing, and recognizing that He had answered them well, asked Him, "What commandment is the foremost of all?" 29 Jesus answered, "The foremost is, 'Hear, O Israel! The Lord our God is one Lord; 30 and you shall love the Lord your God with all your heart, and with all your soul, and with all your mind, and with all your strength.' 31 "The second is this, 'You shall love your neighbor as yourself.' There is no other commandment greater than these." 32 The scribe said to Him, "Right, Teacher; You have truly stated that he is one, and there is no one else besides him; 33 and to love him with all the heart and with all the understanding and with all the strength, and to love one's neighbor as himself, is much more than all burnt offerings and sacrifices."

The Pharisees in the New Testament were careful to follow every religious practice. In the process, they overlooked, the widows, orphans, the ill, and the poverty-stricken. The scribe's statement turns these practices on their head.

So what does this have to do with Christmas? You can have all the right decorations, the best decorated house on the block, and lots of presents under the tree. But this is not what the Lord is seeking from you. You can insist that Christ be kept in Christmas, attend all the church services, and say Merry Christmas to each retail worker as you shop for gifts. Still, this is not what Christ is seeking from you.

On the way to purchase gifts and to participate in church services at Christmas, you pass by widows, orphans, the ill, and impoverished. They struggle to have Christmas at all. Helping them would be to touch a life in a big way. And helping is not as difficult or expensive as it may seem. You can help with a meal, buy a couple gifts to bring a smile to a child's face, help them with small home repairs, or even help put up Christmas decorations. Or perhaps an elderly widow needs a ride to the store or a doctor's appointment. On a more global scale, there are reputable organizations which collect gifts to distribute to very needy children and families.

There are about as many ways to help people in need as you can dream up in your imagination. Don't get me wrong, rituals and decorations are still important. Rituals and decorations provide a certain level of stability and structure. But you must be careful not to lose sight of the importance of other people as you work to make this Christmas the most perfect and memorable ever. Your family will never forget the look on the person's face when you do something unexpected for them. Perhaps this will become a permanent addition to your other favorite Christmas traditions.

## The Christmas Tree

Scripture lesson for December 13th:

Job 38:4-11 Where were you when I laid the foundation of the earth? Tell Me, if you have understanding, 5 Who set its measurements? Since you know. Or who stretched the line on it? 6 On what were its bases sunk? Or who laid its cornerstone, 7 When the morning stars sang together And all the sons of God shouted for joy? 8 Or who enclosed the sea with doors When, bursting forth, it went out from the womb; 9 When I made a cloud its garment And thick darkness its swaddling band, 10 And I placed boundaries on it And set a bolt and doors, 11 And I said, 'Thus far you shall come, but no farther; And here shall your proud waves stop'?

~~~~~~~~~~~~~~~~~~~~~~~~~~~~~~~

There are many different traditions today on bringing a Christmas tree into the home. Some prefer setting up the tree Thanksgiving weekend. Others wait til early December, and still others wait til a few days before Christmas. For some, an artificial tree will do. Others prefer a live tree, and, of them, some buy a tree from a lot, others cut down a tree from a field, and there are a small number of people who go out into the natural hills and mountains to find a tree.

There are a number of different accounts of the history of the Christmas tree, and they make for interesting reading. I encourage you to seek out the history of the tree. Generally, all evergreen trees were revered and sometimes worshipped by ancient cultures. Because it is evergreen, the tree was thought to have mystical powers. And the practice of bringing an evergreen tree into one's house at the winter solstice was begun hundreds of years ago to lift the spirits of the occupants of the home and, in some cases, in an attempt to use the mystical powers of the tree to bring goodwill into the home. Who told the tree to stay green all the time? All the other trees in the forest lose their leaves and are brown and barren in the winter. But the evergreen trees remain green. Who decided that it would be this way?

But rather than focus on the history of the Christmas tree, let's look at some of the features of the tree. First, let's consider the redeeming value of bringing an evergreen tree into the home in the middle of winter. One of my favorite classes in seminary was Contextual Theology, the study and practice of using symbols from the culture as a bridge on which the gospel may cross. Although bringing an evergreen tree into the home may seem like it is built on a pagan tradition, consider that this tradition is a ready-made opportunity to teach the gospel message. The unfortunate reality of American missions abroad is that foreign cultural practices were entirely wiped out because they were viewed as sinful, and the indigenous peoples were forced to subscribe to the American way (or the missionary's way) of relating to the Lord. By taking the time to learn and understand pagan practices, you may actually catch a glimpse of the Lord at work and in the process be able to share this view of the Lord with the unbelievers. American mission movements have begun to approach foreign cultures in this way, and hopefully the practice continues.

Looking at the tree itself, take note of its important features – evergreen, triangular shape, arrow pointing upward, many branches, and, of course, the tree itself. Just as the Christmas tree is evergreen, the Lord is everlasting. The triangular shape can be used to describe the Trinity – God the Father, God the Son and God the Holy Spirit – and, just as the tree is many branches yet held together as a unit consisting of the whole tree, God is three persons yet one God. The pointed shape of the tree draws your attention upward, as if it is an arrow directing you to look up into the heavens. The tall spires of churches, especially in cities, are also meant to draw your attention upward for the same reason. The many branches of the tree can be used to symbolize the church. This could be done in several different ways. One approach may be to use each needle to represent individual people and then each branch to represent a different church. The junctions in the branches can be used to teach church history. All churches are then connected to the trunk, Jesus Christ our Lord. All the needles connect to the trunk through the diversity of the branches, and one particular needle is not better than another.

More importantly, Christ is sometimes referred to as having been crucified on a tree. Certainly the cross was made of wood and was derived from a tree or several trees. Let this Christmas season be a reminder to you that through Christ's death on the cross your salvation was made possible. Take this time to remember and to be thankful for what He has done for you. Also, be thankful that the Lord ever seeks you out and pursues you. If He did not, we would all be in deep trouble of cosmic proportions.

As you bring the Christmas tree into your home this season, take a moment to discuss with your family – and your friends – the many different ways the tree symbolizes Christ at work in the world and in your own life. Perhaps you will even find an opportunity to witness to some unbelieving friends in a new way.

## Decorative Lights at Christmas

Scripture lesson for December 14th:

Psalm 18:28 For You light my lamp; The LORD my God illumines my darkness. Matthew 4:16 The people who were sitting in darkness saw a great light, and those who were sitting in the land and shadow of death, upon them a light dawned." Matthew 5:14-16 You are the light of the world. A city set on a hill cannot be hidden; 15 nor does anyone light a lamp and put it under a basket, but on the lampstand, and it gives light to all who are in the house. 16 Let your light shine before men in such a way that they may see your good works, and glorify your Father who is in heaven.

~~~~~~~~~~~~~~~~~~~~~~~~~~~~~~

Throughout Scripture there is a theme of the Lord representing light and sin representing darkness. This is somewhat of a practical image because all light displaces darkness, and wherever light shines, darkness cannot prevail. You can see from the Scripture for today where the childhood church song This Little Light of Mine originated from. This is a beautiful song because it not only represents light but also represents sharing light and letting it shine into a dark world.

Perhaps unknowingly, churchgoers often sing of light in popular Christmas hymns – *Do You Hear What I Hear*, *Hark the Herald Angels Sing*, *O Holy Night*, *O Little Town of Bethlehem*, *Silent Night*, and *We Three Kings* to name a few.

According to Ace Collins, the practice of decorating the Christmas tree with lights seems to have originated from Martin Luther, probably in the 1500s. While it would seem Luther used the lights more for decoration at first, there are a few records which seem to indicate that he also used the decorative light to teach the gospel and to tell of God's marvelous works in creation.

If you have light – The Light – your desire should be to illuminate the world. And at Christmas time some people do just that – literally. The decorations are very nice and beautiful to behold. But do the lights strung on

Christmas trees and homes actually represent anything meaningful? To the stores that sell lights, they represent profit. But perhaps this year you can use decorative lights to shine your light into a dark world.

Light under a basket (or a bushel) serves no useful purpose. The purpose of light is to illuminate an area, usually a room or a small part of the yard or parking lot. So tell the world you have the gospel and are prepared to share it. Let your light shine into a dark world.

And make sure there are no obstructions blocking your light. The more light shines in your heart, the more light will shine from your life.

Today, spend some time in prayer inviting the Lord to search your heart to see if there is any place in the rooms of your heart that light cannot shine and then invite Him to help you remove the obstruction. The Lord's light should illuminate *all* of your heart and not just a few areas that you pre-select.

## Hungry for Food, Starving for the Gospel

Scripture lesson for December 15th:

1 Kings 17:9-24 "Arise, go to Zarephath, which belongs to Sidon, and stay there; behold, I have commanded a widow there to provide for you." 10 So he arose and went to Zarephath, and when he came to the gate of the city, behold, a widow was there gathering sticks; and he called to her and said, "Please get me a little water in a jar, that I may drink." 11 As she was going to get it, he called to her and said, "Please bring me a piece of bread in your hand." 12 But she said, "As the LORD your God lives, I have no bread, only a handful of flour in the bowl and a little oil in the jar; and behold, I am gathering a few sticks that I may go in and prepare for me and my son, that we may eat it and die." 13 Then Elijah said to her, "Do not fear; go, do as you have said, but make me a little bread cake from it first and bring it out to me, and afterward you may make one for yourself and for your son. 14 "For thus says the LORD God of Israel, 'The bowl of flour shall not be exhausted, nor shall the jar of oil be empty, until the day that the LORD sends rain on the face of the earth.'" 15 So she went and did according to the word of Elijah, and she and he and her household ate for many days. 16 The bowl of flour was not exhausted nor did the jar of oil become empty, according to the word of the LORD which He spoke through Elijah. 17 Now it came about after these things that the son of the woman, the mistress of the house, became sick; and his sickness was so severe that there was no breath left in him. 18 So she said to Elijah, "What do I have to do with you, O man of God? You have come to me to bring my iniquity to remembrance and to put my son to death!" 19 He said to her, "Give me your son." Then he took him from her bosom and carried him up to the upper room where he was living, and laid him on his own bed. 20 He called to the LORD and said, "O LORD my God, have You also brought calamity to the widow with whom I am staying, by causing her son to die?" 21 Then he stretched himself upon the child three times, and called to the LORD and said, "O LORD my God, I pray You, let this child's life return to him." 22 The LORD heard the voice of Elijah, and the life of the child returned to him and he revived. 23 Elijah took the child and brought him down from the upper room into the house and gave him to his mother; and Elijah said, "See, your son is alive." 24 Then the woman said to Elijah, "Now I know that you are a man of God and that the word of the LORD in your mouth is truth."

~~~~~~~~~~~~~~~~~~~~~~~~~~~~~~

Perhaps today's Scripture lesson sounds familiar to you. Your scarce resources are stretched beyond their limits. And just as soon as one good thing happens to you, another tragedy strikes which causes yet another setback.

Nothing happens in this life which goes unnoticed by the Lord. He saw the plight of the widow and her son, the same way he sees your plight and the circumstances of the poor, the widows and the orphans. The Lord provided for the widow woman, and He met her immediate physical needs. She probably had a long list of "wants." But the Lord did not create you to be dependent on Him for everything. Sometimes you have to trust that the Lord is meeting your most pressing needs and that you should not focus on your wants. In fact, your wants can sometimes cloud your relationship with the Lord. Your wants have a tendency to become idols. Your wants can also distract you from the tasks the Lord has set before you. That is not to say your wants are unimportant to the Lord. But He expects that you put the importance of His heavenly kingdom ahead of your wants and desires. How different would things be today if Martin Luther, John Wesley, George Muller, Mother Theresa, Amy Carmichael, Jim Elliott, and Dwight Moody – to name a few – had put their wants ahead of the kingdom?

At one time or other, they had immediate, pressing physical and bodily needs. But they leaned on the Lord for those needs and had them met. No doubt they also had their various wants and desires. But they laid aside those wants and desires for the sake of the Kingdom of Heaven. Paul instructs you to do the same in Hebrews 12:1-2:

> Therefore, since we have so great a cloud of witnesses surrounding us, let us also lay aside every encumbrance and the sin which so easily entangles us, and let us run with endurance the race that is set before us, 2 fixing our eyes on Jesus, the author and perfecter of faith, who for the joy set before Him endured the cross, despising the shame, and has sat down at the right hand of the throne of God.

The Lord has His own priorities. Although the widow needed to eat, she also needed to know who the Lord was, and it took a miracle in the kitchen to open her heart to a relationship with the Lord.

This Christmas, fix your eyes on Jesus. Lay aside every encumbrance, anything which weighs you down, and any sin, which easily entangles you and gear up with endurance. Although I like how Paul compares the walk with Christ to a race, I do not believe you should get caught up in the idea of competition. Rather, I believe your focus should be on finishing the race honorably. Still, I encourage you not to lose sight of your wants and desires. But this Christmas, as you focus on Christ, I believe you will find that you will be blessed in ways you could never have imagined and that you will be much more satisfied than if you had gotten everything you wanted.

Today, make a list of your top five wants and desires. At the bottom of the list, write out a brief prayer about the things on the list. Then, put that list somewhere safe, such as your sock drawer or fire safe, and leave it there for at least six months. When the things on the list come to mind, say a short prayer over the list. This will leave you with the ability to focus on your most pressing needs, while not abandoning the other things that matter to you.

## A Message for the Broken Hearted

Scripture lesson for December 16th:

Psalm 34:1b-16 I will bless the LORD at all times; His praise shall continually be in my mouth. 2 My soul will make its boast in the LORD; The humble will hear it and rejoice. 3 O magnify the LORD with me, And let us exalt His name together. 4 I sought the LORD, and He answered me, And delivered me from all my fears. 5 They looked to Him and were radiant, And their faces will never be ashamed. 6 This poor man cried, and the LORD heard him And saved him out of all his troubles. 7 The angel of the LORD encamps around those who fear Him, And rescues them. 8 O taste and see that the LORD is good; How blessed is the man who takes refuge in Him! 9 O fear the LORD, you His saints; For to those who fear Him there is no want. 10 The young lions do lack and suffer hunger; But they who seek the LORD shall not be in want of any good thing. 11 Come, you children, listen to me; I will teach you the fear of the LORD. 12 Who is the man who desires life And loves length of days that he may see good? 13 Keep your tongue from evil And your lips from speaking deceit. 14 Depart from evil and do good; Seek peace and pursue it. 15 The eyes of the LORD are toward the righteous And His ears are open to their cry. 16 The face of the LORD is against evildoers, To cut off the memory of them from the earth. Matthew 10:29-31 Are not two sparrows sold for a cent? And yet not one of them will fall to the ground apart from your Father. 30 But the very hairs of your head are all numbered. 31 So do not fear; you are more valuable than many sparrows.

~~~~~~~~~~~~~~~~~~~~~~~~~~~~~~~

Christmas is a very special time of the year. Unfortunately, Christmas does not hold the same excitement and allure for the broken hearted. This may be a first or another Christmas without a spouse; a child; a parent; or even a best friend. A close family member may be seriously ill or even in the hospital. A marriage may be on the brink of divorce, or a friendship or family relationship may be strained over a disagreement, hurtful incident or misunderstanding. The family income may have been drastically cut or a job was totally lost due to economic difficulties.

The world is not a kind place. Disease, dementia, crime, accidents around the home, frustration, injustice, oppression, and heartache in relationships are all lurking in the world around you. Sometimes, the circumstances of life can become so difficult that it seems the Lord is far away and slow to intervene.

In today's Scripture lesson, David sought the Lord and cried to the Lord. The Lord answered David and delivered him, and the Lord heard David and saved him. This is David's personal testimony to you about his experience with the Lord. David invites you to look to the Lord, and you will never be ashamed. He invites you to let the Lord set up His angels around you to rescue you. He invites you to taste and see that the Lord is good. He invites you to take refuge in Him. Hear the invitations of David. Have an attitude of awe and reverence toward the Lord and have a daily diet of the Bible.

It is unfortunate that some have interpreted David's promise that those who fear the Lord will not want (see also Psalm 23) to mean that they will prosper financially. But this is not what David says. If you depend only on the world and this life for the things you need and for relief from your circumstances and your heartache, you will be disappointed. If you believe that a long, full life is what matters, you will again be disappointed. David uses the irony of the young lions going hungry to prove his point. Young lions are among the most self-sufficient creates on the earth. Yet, self-sufficiency is not the attitude the Lord can use to meet your needs and address your situation.

It may be true that some who have depended on the Lord will have financial prosperity. But financial prosperity must not be the focus of your attention or even your end goal. All that matters in this life is that you are right with the Lord. After all, there is no record that anyone has been able to take their possessions with them when they die. Some have tried, but even they were unsuccessful.

Jesus reaffirms the instruction and testimony of David that those who have reverence for the Lord and place their trust in the Lord will share in the Lord's providence. But notice again that Jesus takes your attention away from financial prosperity. Even sparrows fall on hard times, yet they are important enough to the Lord that every sparrow that falls catches His attention. If He knows when a single sparrow falls and you are much more valuable to Him than a sparrow, then most certainly He knows of your difficulties.

Taste and see that the Lord is good. His body was broken for you on the cross. His blood was shed for your salvation. Try Him today and see if He will not send His angels to rescue you. Take refuge in Him and you will not be ashamed. This Christmas, celebrate the anticipation of the return of the One who issues these promises. Celebrate the anticipation of meeting Him face to face.

Today, spend some time in prayer to lay your circumstances before the Lord. Do this each day for the next 30 days, and at the end of 30 days see what direction and comfort the Lord has for you.

## Angels Unaware

Scripture lesson for December 17th:

Hebrews 13:1-3 Let love of the brethren continue. 2 Do not neglect to show hospitality to strangers for by this some have entertained angels without knowing it. 3 Remember the prisoners, as though in prison with them, and those who are ill-treated, since you yourselves also are in the body.

~~~~~~~~~~~~~~~~~~~~~~~~~~~~~

Ace Collins writes of the legend of St. Nicholas, who has become Santa Claus, and that he was born in the fourth century to wealthy parents who died when he was still young. He gave his parents' wealth away to the needy of his village and entered into the Christian ministry as a monk, to later become an archbishop. A particular story which has been passed down through the generations is that a poor widower had three daughters. He wanted his daughters to marry and live apart from his poverty, but he had no money to pay the dowry as was the custom at that time. Word of his poverty came to St. Nicholas who wanted to help but be anonymous in the process. The legend goes that he devised a plan to enter the house at night through an open window while the family was sleeping and leave gold coins in the oldest girl's stockings which hung from the hearth to dry.

Of course, the girl and her father were elated at the discovery the next morning. As the two other girls matured to marrying age, St. Nicholas did the same for them. The legend continues that as the villagers learned of the great gifts, they soon engaged in the practice of leaving a window open and stockings hung from the hearth. With St. Nicholas' gifts to this particular family and his other acts of generosity with his parents' wealth in distributing it to the needy, he earned great notoriety.

Although this is described by historians as a legend, I believe there are at least some kernels of truth in these stories. After all, the colors of red, green and gold, the use of holly and other evergreens to decorate the home, Christmas trees, lights on Christmas trees, trimming trees and decorations, and even Yule logs all originated from documented events in history.

But St. Nicholas has long since passed away, and his wealth has all been distributed. It is inconceivable that his spirit lives on in Santa Claus as modern commercialism would have you believe. However, the spirit of his generosity does indeed live on today and for all time. What you may not know is that the original image of modern day Santa Claus was depicted as giving gifts to the poor. It was commercialism that turned him into the visitor of the well to do homes. This made it difficult for everyone to believe in Santa Claus because Santa never came to a family who was very poor and could not afford a new bicycle, riding toy or other special toy a child wanted.

The circumstance of those who do not enjoy the things others have come to take for granted in their daily lives must not be forgotten. At this very moment and even this Christmas, there are children who will go hungry, who are homeless, who are orphans and who will not receive for Christmas the one special toy they hoped for all year long. There are adults and parents who are without a job, who have a job but earn less than they need to pay their bills, and who cannot afford to pay for needed medical care for themselves, a family member or even a child. These problems occur on a regular basis in your own backyard, and they are even more acute in certain areas around the world.

That fateful evening on which Santa Claus claims his origin, St. Nicholas ministered to a poor family. He did something for them which they otherwise could not do for themselves.

This Christmas, seek out the story and history of Santa Claus and tell it to your children, grandchildren or the children in your life.

## Slowing Down

Scripture lesson for December 18th:

Luke 10:38-42 Now as they were traveling along, He entered a village; and a woman named Martha welcomed Him into her home. 39 She had a sister called Mary, who was seated at the Lord's feet, listening to His word. 40 But Martha was distracted with all her preparations; and she came up to Him and said, "Lord, do You not care that my sister has left me to do all the serving alone? Then tell her to help me." 41 But the Lord answered and said to her, "Martha, Martha, you are worried and bothered about so many things; 42 but only one thing is necessary, for Mary has chosen the good part, which shall not be taken away from her."

~~~~~~~~~~~~~~~~~~~~~~~~~~~~~

I do not believe I am alone in saying that there are certain traditions I feel must be honored to have the perfect Christmas. I am also not alone in believing that having just the right feeling and just the right mood makes Christmas the most meaningful and special time of year. Visiting with family, traveling, snow, a real tree, decorations, fire in the fireplace, and Christmas ham are just a few traditions many people – myself included – try to keep to have the perfect Christmas.

All too soon, however, Christmas is over, and if you are not careful you will have missed the significance and meaning of this season. If I don't have the right feeling about Christmas and if it goes by too quickly, then I feel I have been robbed! I prefer to savor every moment and to help instill and build traditions with my children that they can enjoy and pass down to their children.

I have had the opportunity recently to hear the advice of radio personalities offering encouragement and empowerment to take a deep breath and slow down to enjoy the holidays. It is certainly true that you can get so caught up in preparing for Christmas that you don't have time to enjoy it – shopping for gifts, driving through traffic, getting groceries for parties and family meals, cooking and cleaning up. Although those things have their own redeeming values and can be part of lasting traditions, these tasks can also take away from Christmas.

It is almost as if you can become so busy preparing for Christmas that you miss it entirely! In the Scripture lesson for today, it would appear that Martha was so busy preparing for Jesus to arrive and to eat with Him that she missed His visit entirely! Mary, on the other hand, did not worry that everything had to be just right or that dirty dishes were sitting waiting to be washed and put away. The moments spent with Jesus were irreplaceable and had to be savored while they lasted. Preparations need not be formal. Dirty dishes will still be there. But for now, the anticipation and excitement of time with Jesus were too much to be spent working in the kitchen.

My desire at Christmas is to take the time to enjoy it, to let the excitement build and then to be captivated by every moment spent with my family and in community worship at church. One of my traditions while Christmas shopping is to get a hot soft pretzel. It may seem trivial, but I find that it gives me time to sit down and shut down in the middle of the store or the mall and to remind myself to take it slow and to savor every moment.

Don't let this Christmas get by you without warning. Take it slow, enjoy the moment. This season is not marked by preparations. Rather, it is marked by anticipation. After all, there is nothing you can do to clean yourself up to meet Jesus. If there were, you wouldn't need him. No, you do not have the power within yourself to meet his standards and requirements. You can only come to the Lord in your wretched state, your casual place settings at the table, meals cooked in your everyday pots and pans, and dirty dishes sitting in the sink. Once you have had time to spend with the Lord, you will find that the mess is not as difficult to clean up as you expected because for now you have Christ in you to guide your pathways. And Christmas is much more than just anticipation. It is the excitement of the day – the day when you meet Jesus!

Would I want my home to be spic and span for a visit from Jesus? Absolutely. But I also know that if I spend my time preparing and cleaning myself up while he is here, I will miss that special time with and all too soon my time with Him will come to a close, for I can't live on the mountaintops each day – if I did, I would never experience the adversity in life which always teaches me (and you) to depend more on Christ. So why not make the most of it while you have that special time together? This Christmas, take it slow; anticipate the excitement; and then savor each exciting moment. The memory of the special moments spent together with family – and with Christ – will carry you through the valleys in life.

Today, invite the Lord to calm your spirit, give you the strength to enjoy the season, and the courage to face any difficulties or conflict you are expecting.

## Materialism

Scripture lesson for December 19th:

Luke 12:15-25 Then He said to them, "Beware, and be on your guard against every form of greed; for not even when one has an abundance does his life consist of his possessions." 16 And He told them a parable, saying, "The land of a rich man was very productive. 17 "And he began reasoning to himself, saying, 'What shall I do, since I have no place to store my crops?' 18 "Then he said, 'This is what I will do: I will tear down my barns and build larger ones, and there I will store all my grain and my goods. 19 'And I will say to my soul, "Soul, you have many goods laid up for many years to come; take your ease, eat, drink and be merry."' 20 "But God said to him, 'You fool! This very night your soul is required of you; and now who will own what you have prepared?' 21 "So is the man who stores up treasure for himself, and is not rich toward God." 22 And He said to His disciples, "For this reason I say to you, do not worry about your life, as to what you will eat; nor for your body, as to what you will put on. 23 "For life is more than food, and the body more than clothing. 24 "Consider the ravens, for they neither sow nor reap; they have no storeroom nor barn, and yet God feeds them; how much more valuable you are than the birds! 25 "And which of you by worrying can add a single hour to his life's span?

~~~~~~~~~~~~~~~~~~~~~~~~~~~~~~

What is under your tree this Christmas? Materialism is a very difficult subject, and it is even more touchy at Christmas. It is the one time of year parents enjoy spoiling their children, spouses go all out for each other, grandparents lavish on their grandchildren, and friends try to find that perfect gift or even out-give someone else.

Christmas presents themselves are not inherently wrong or bad just as harvesting and storing are not wrong. In today's Scripture lesson, a farmer is harvesting his fields and storing his grain. In fact, in Genesis 41:34-49, Joseph stored up large amounts of grain for seven years. So how can anyone say that storing grain is evil? And Psalm 24:1 says that the whole earth is the Lord's and everything in it. It would be preposterous that the Creator of the universe *needs* farmers to limit how much they store, so He has enough excess grain to feed the hungry! If the Lord's grain supply depended on each farmer, then the Lord isn't what the Bible has made Him out to be.

So what was this farmer's crime? From reading today's lesson closely, there seem to be two crimes – first, the farmer elected to hoard his harvest instead of giving it to the Lord to be distributed to the poor, the fatherless, the orphans and the widows, and second, the farmer believed his future existence depended only on his own work. Selfishness and idolatry are at the heart of materialism.

This farmer was rich in earthly goods but poor in spiritual matters. Is it possible to be absurdly wealthy yet exist in abject poverty? In Revelation 3:17, this same contrast is used – wealthy yet poor. Materialism breeds emptiness, a feeling that something is missing, and a mistaken belief that, if the abundance of things is all there is, then maybe life just isn't worth living.

So what do the gifts under your Christmas tree this year say about you? Remember, gifts themselves are not inherently evil. Perhaps you should start by asking yourself this question – does my self-worth and self-image and that of my children depend on the things under the tree? A television commercial once advertised that buying the product would go beyond keeping up with the Joneses, it would turn you into the Joneses. You know the Joneses, right? They are the family in the cul-de-sac in suburbia with all the latest and greatest stuff. They set the trends, they have life all figured out, and they are so very happy because they are on top of the world. Everyone wants to be like them. People have gone bankrupt trying to keep up with the Joneses.

Another question to ask is whether you have made provisions to give to the poor, the fatherless, the orphans and the widows. These days, you do not need to go far to find people who are hurting and who are in need. The farmer may have been commended if he had given away his excess, the share of the harvest which did not fit into his existing storage facilities. But even then, he would have violated the Lord's command to give Him your first fruits, your best because he was only giving the leftovers.

Jesus makes an interesting point in today's lesson, one that is worth serious consideration. Consider the birds, He says, because they do not plant in the spring and harvest in the fall, and they do not have anywhere to store their goods. Still, the Lord feeds them.

Your very existence, indeed your purpose in life, depends on the Lord. Stuff – material things – is like a dirty windshield on your car – after awhile, it gets to the point when you just can't see well enough to know where you are and where you are going. Stuff – and focusing on materialism – creates a situation which tends to cloud your understanding of the fact that *you* depend on the Lord. It distracts you from focusing on the Lord, and it deprives you of becoming the person the Lord intended you to be.

Today, invite the Lord to examine your heart and to show you any area in which you treasure the things of this world more than Him. Where your treasure is, there also will your heart be.

## The Smallest Gift

Scripture lesson for December 20th:

Acts 3:1-8 Now Peter and John were going up to the temple at the ninth hour, the hour of prayer. 2 And a man who had been lame from his mother's womb was being carried along, whom they used to set down every day at the gate of the temple which is called Beautiful, in order to beg alms of those who were entering the temple. 3 When he saw Peter and John about to go into the temple, he began asking to receive alms. 4 But Peter, along with John, fixed his gaze on him and said, "Look at us!" 5 And he began to give them his attention, expecting to receive something from them. 6 But Peter said, "I do not possess silver and gold, but what I do have I give to you: In the name of Jesus Christ the Nazarene—walk!" 7 And seizing him by the right hand, he raised him up; and immediately his feet and his ankles were strengthened. 8 With a leap he stood upright and began to walk; and he entered the temple with them, walking and leaping and praising God.

~~~~~~~~~~~~~~~~~~~~~~~~~~~~~

To this point I have tried to keep stories about myself to a minimum and focus instead on Christ at work in the world. So now a word of warning to you – today's reading is a story from my childhood, and I trust it will be an encouragement to you.

In the mid-1980s, I was a child, and we lived in a northern Pennsylvania farm house. It was a two-story yellow house with a sprawling front porch, and to me, anyway, it was old but intriguing. We did not farm the land but only rented the house, although the farmer always left some corn in the fields that we gleaned for corn meal, corn bread, corn mush, and anything else with corn in it. It was a time of transition for our family since my father had moved us there to pursue dreams of his that were not yet meant to take shape. Anyway, we did not have much money, in fact, for several months after moving into the house we did not have a telephone. Ice cream was a treat once in a great while.

I have many fond memories of the house for the short time we lived there, and one stands out in particular. I wondered how my parents would handle

Christmas because we did not have much money. On Christmas morning, I came downstairs, and sure enough there were not many gifts under the tree. One of them was a Matchbox Peterbilt milk truck. The truck cab was blue, and the tank was white with the word "milk" in red letters. Because it was one of a few gifts my parents gave me that year, it was my prized possession! I enjoyed that truck so much and played with it all the time.

I was home-schooled, and at the time my parents were local coordinators for our home-schooling program, which meant sometimes other parents would come to our house for a few hours to speak with my parents. One day, one such family came with their little boy who was about my age but very rambunctious. I let him play with my toys, but it was not til after they left that I noticed he had broken the headlights off my new milk truck!! I was devastated and angry. I almost threw it away thinking I could never play with it again because it was broken.

I still have the milk truck, and once in awhile I get it out and use it as an example of several things. You are God's prized possession, and Jesus treasures little children. In life, it is all too easy to be broken by other people or by circumstances. The Lord doesn't throw you away! In fact, you never lose your status with Him as His prized possession! Read today's Scripture lesson again. Here was a broken, forgotten man who lived on the little other people threw his way. How ironic that though he was lame and probably not someone you would enjoy looking at, yet he sat at the Beautiful gate. As broken as he was, this man was the Lord's prized possession, and to demonstrate it, the Lord healed him! You are not forgotten by the Lord nor does He cast you aside just because you may be broken.

If my milk truck had feelings, it would probably feel shame because it was broken and afraid it would lose its status with me because of what it had been through and because it had been broken. You may have feelings of shame before the Lord and sometimes other people. But the Lord in His infinite grace and mercy looks beyond your shame and your brokenness and continues to seek to have a relationship with you, no matter how broken you are.

More importantly, the Matchbox Peterbilt milk truck serves as a reminder to me of a time that was very instrumental in my later coming to Christ. It was the acts of kindness of others in our church which sometimes kept food on our table and a roof over our heads that were instrumental in forming my faith in the Lord. When a person performs an act of kindness for someone else, they may not realize it in the moment, but they are bringing the reality of the Lord into someone's life – just like Peter and John did to the lame man by the Beautiful gate. And maybe the person receiving the act of kindness will turn to Christ in their time of brokenness, and, of course, He is there, waiting with open arms. This milk truck is much more than a toy to me. It is a constant reminder that beauty can indeed rise out of the ashes of brokenness. You are beautiful to the Lord no matter how broken you think you are.

Today, allow the Lord to examine your brokenness and shame. Allow yourself to be vulnerable before Him. The Lord has promised to treat you gently. Let yourself slip into His outstretched arms and find your much needed rest and acceptance there.

## Thriving in the Harsh Winter

Scripture lesson for December 21st:

Psalm 23:1-6 A Psalm of David. The LORD is my shepherd, I shall not want. 2 He makes me lie down in green pastures; He leads me beside quiet waters. 3 He restores my soul; He guides me in the paths of righteousness For His name's sake. 4 Even though I walk through the valley of the shadow of death, I fear no evil, for You are with me; Your rod and Your staff, they comfort me. 5 You prepare a table before me in the presence of my enemies; You have anointed my head with oil; My cup overflows. 6 Surely goodness and lovingkindness will follow me all the days of my life, And I will dwell in the house of the LORD forever.
Zechariah 13:9 "And I will bring the third part through the fire, Refine them as silver is refined, And test them as gold is tested. They will call on My name, And I will answer them; I will say, 'They are My people,' And they will say, 'The LORD is my God.'"

~~~~~~~~~~~~~~~~~~~~~~~~~~~~~~

Today is the common day for the winter solstice, and one of the most intriguing historical accounts I came across while studying the history and origin of the many Christmas traditions is that of the holly tree. Holly is an evergreen tree which bears small, red berries. Centuries ago, holly was revered as mystical and magical because of its ability to survive and stay green during the harshest winter conditions. But this is not the primary reason holly was revered because there are many, many other evergreen trees and plants which survive in the harsh winter. The first known account of magic associated with the holly tree indicates that people were mystified because it bore fruit – small, red berries – in the winter snow and freezing temperatures. This is very mystifying because nothing was capable of surviving in the cold winters, much less bear fruit!

You may not realize it, but, as a Christian, growth and strength are often related with difficult times. A very short summary of the Christian Bible is that the Bible prepares you for your life with Christ after you die. To become more Christ-like, the Bible teaches you to abandon sin, accept the sacrifice of Christ as atonement for your sin, and to embody the example of Christ in prayer, fasting, teaching, evangelism, and kindness to others. But

Christ also forewarns you (and me) and even promises that you will endure hardship, temptation, difficulty and even persecution and ridicule.

It is during these hard times that you, like the account of Job in the Old Testament, must rely on Christ for strength and deliverance. It is often a time of testing your faith in Christ. Do you believe He will be there when you need Him?

When you enter the winter-times of your life, you often do not know what lies ahead. As you place your trust in Christ to see you through, you will thrive, just like the holly. But more than this, if you take a closer look at those difficult times in your life, no doubt you will notice that fruit was born out of difficulty. The most common example of people bearing fruit in difficult times is that of persecution. Or how about people noticing the light on your face and your positive attitude even while enduring cancer, the loss of a child, a tough day at work, the loss of a long-term relationship, a house fire. People do not miss your reaction and ability to survive those hardships, just like our ancestors could not miss the red berries on the evergreen holly contrasting against the cold, harsh white snow and dark, bare trees. In the season of barrenness, life is much more visible. Who has been touched by you in your difficult seasons? You were certainly all touched by Christ through His difficulty – His death on the cross for you and for your sins.

Today, take some time to prayerfully reflect on days gone by and especially difficult times. Then invite the Lord to show you how He was at work and what fruit came from those times.

## A Lesson from St. Nicholas

Scripture lesson for December 22nd:

Matthew 25:35-40 For I was hungry, and you gave Me something to eat; I was thirsty, and you gave Me something to drink; I was a stranger, and you invited Me in; 36 naked, and you clothed Me; I was sick, and you visited Me; I was in prison, and you came to Me. 37 Then the righteous will answer Him, 'Lord, when did we see You hungry, and feed You, or thirsty, and give You something to drink? 38 And when did we see You a stranger, and invite You in, or naked, and clothe You? 39 When did we see You sick, or in prison, and come to You?' 40 The King will answer and say to them, 'Truly I say to you, to the extent that you did it to one of these brothers of Mine, even the least of them, you did it to Me.'

~~~~~~~~~~~~~~~~~~~~~~~~~~~~~~

It has often been said that followers of Christ should embody Jesus Christ in helping other people. When you perform an act of kindness for people in need, you are Jesus to them. I for one struggle with this image. Before you rush to judgment, I am not advocating that you stop helping the poor. But I am saying that perhaps the ones who promote this message have it wrong.

In the Scripture lesson for today, Jesus makes some rather pointed statements – I was hungry; I was thirsty; I was a stranger; I was naked; I was sick; I was in prison. The "righteous" were bewildered! Jesus was none of those things. He was divine! There are no records that Jesus was ever imprisoned. And He made all things in the earth. He turned water into wine and a few loaves and fish into a meal sufficient to feed 5,000 – with leftovers. How unimaginable that the Creator of the universe would be hungry or thirsty!

Rather than you as His follower embodying the example of Christ, Jesus here says that you are to serve Him, not embody Him. In serving the "least" of people, you are serving Jesus Christ Himself. Can there be a more honorable task than to serve the Creator of the universe? And by the way, the next time someone says you should be Jesus to someone in need, ask them if they have ever created a universe. That would be a preposterous notion, wouldn't it? Think about it ... either you can serve the Creator of the universe in love and humility or you can become the Creator of the universe so that you can serve others in pride and arrogance.

If you ask me, I'd much rather serve the Creator of the universe than to make a feeble attempt at embodying Him.

Should you be doing works in Jesus' name? Yes, I believe so. You should always represent Jesus Christ well in the world. But should you think you are better than other people such that you can embody Jesus Christ just so that you can serve them? St. Nicholas did not think so. He wanted to remain anonymous, not boast that he was being Jesus to someone in need. I believe whether you are Jesus to someone or whether you serve Jesus in meeting the needs of people in a hurting world is a matter of orientation and how you view yourself in the world. St. Nicholas chose the route of serving people.

Now consider this story, the story of *Papa Panov's Special Christmas* by Leo Tolstoy. Panov has a dream in which he believes he hears Jesus Himself tell him that He is coming tomorrow. Panov anticipates Jesus coming to his shop. By the end of the day, all that he had seen were an old man shoveling snow to whom he gave a warm cup of tea, a soldier's wife who was homeless, unemployed, and passing through town on her way to another village to look for work, to whom he gave a place to rest, a warm coat and a small meal, and then a boy caught stealing an apple from a widow woman on her way home from the market, and Panov intervened on the boy's behalf to mediate an amicable resolution. At the end of the day, Panov is tired and disappointed, he lays down to rest and in another dream hears a voice that simply says, "I came today." Panov awakes to argue with Jesus, saying that he never saw Jesus. But then Panov is reminded of the three people he helped that day, and it was plain to see that Jesus had come in the form of a stranger.

An argument can be made that Panov was Jesus to these three strangers. Yet, what makes Panov any better than they? And Panov did not seek them out; each one of the strangers came to Panov. What Panov did was respond to a need, much the same as St. Nicholas did. Even Jesus responded to needs. There were few if any times that Jesus just acted to meet a need. Jesus always made the person tell Him what they needed before He would give it to them. If you embody Jesus Christ, are you responding to a need or are you taking away the responsibility of the person in need to ask? The implications of the answer to that question are far reaching.

Consider this challenge: Next time you see a person in need, assume that it is Jesus Himself who has the need. How are you going to minister to Jesus? The "righteous" in the Scripture lesson today were quick to say that if only they had seen *Jesus* seeking food, drink, clothing, shelter and visitation, they would have responded instantaneously. What they failed to realize is that, since they did not see *Jesus* in the circumstances of the needy families, they were neglecting to care for the poor, the orphans, the homeless and the widows – and anyone else who is stuck in the margins of society. Do you really feel comfortable advocating such a legalistic opinion at the second coming of Jesus Christ, or would you agree that the spirit of the law is such that you should reach out to everyone who is in need regardless of the race, gender, background or divine affiliation?

## Watching for Him

Scripture lesson for December 23rd:

Matthew 25:1-13 Then the kingdom of heaven will be comparable to ten virgins, who took their lamps and went out to meet the bridegroom. 2 Five of them were foolish, and five were prudent. 3 For when the foolish took their lamps, they took no oil with them, 4 but the prudent took oil in flasks along with their lamps. 5 Now while the bridegroom was delaying, they all got drowsy and began to sleep. 6 But at midnight there was a shout, 'Behold, the bridegroom! Come out to meet him.' 7 Then all those virgins rose and trimmed their lamps. 8 The foolish said to the prudent, 'Give us some of your oil, for our lamps are going out.' 9 But the prudent answered, 'No, there will not be enough for us and you too; go instead to the dealers and buy some for yourselves.' 10 And while they were going away to make the purchase, the bridegroom came, and those who were ready went in with him to the wedding feast; and the door was shut. 11 Later the other virgins also came, saying, 'Lord, lord, open up for us.' 12 But he answered, 'Truly I say to you, I do not know you.' 13 Be on the alert then, for you do not know the day nor the hour.

~~~~~~~~~~~~~~~~~~~~~~~~~~~~~~

This Christmas, as in years past, children all over will watch in longing expectation for Santa Claus to come. No doubt *The Night Before Christmas* will be read in many homes, and children will again wonder if this time he will come, landing on the roof and creating such a clatter. This Christmas Eve, families will also no doubt sit around the tree watching for the clock to strike midnight, celebrating the return of Christmas for another year.

Throughout both the Old and New Testaments of the Bible, watching is a very important duty. Some of today's children are taught to watch for Santa Claus. Some even teach their children that behavior influences what Santa Claus does for them. In the military, watching – especially during the night – is a very important task. Ship captains establish a night watch on the bridge. Campers out in the open country air often set up night watches. Hospitals also keep a certain number of doctors and nurses on staff during the night after the primary doctors have gone home to rest. Prison guards stand watch over their inmates. And today, homes have security systems which are monitored.

In the Bible, there are some very important reasons to watch. Deuteronomy 4:23 says to watch that you keep the covenant of the Lord. Guarding your heart from evil and wrongdoing is a very important reason to keep watch. In today's Scripture lesson, you see that it is also important to watch to stay alert and be ready for the day of the Lord's coming.

When you watch, it is more difficult to be taken by surprise. You can be forewarned of potential attacks. You can address situations which arise before they get out of hand. But what happens when you see potential threats on the horizon? If you are not armed or do not have a way to communicate to the camp, you are left having no way to prepare, and the threat will be upon you by the time you are ready to deal with it.

If the arrival of Santa Claus depends upon a child's behavior, then the time to watch that behavior begins on December 26th! If the child only began to watch on December 24th, it will be too late! Likewise, it is important that you keep the covenant of the Lord and that you begin your watch as soon as possible and continue it moment to moment.

Today's Scripture lesson also says to watch in longing expectation for the second coming of Christ. The problem with the one group was that they were not prepared. I live in Florida and have been through several major hurricanes. This Scripture lesson is akin to me saying in the middle of a night-time hurricane that I ran out of batteries for my flashlight. Certainly, this would be the time when I need my flashlight the most because in the middle of the storm the electricity would be cut off from my home due to damaged power lines. Stores would be closed, so there would be nowhere to buy batteries. And at the moment I step outside, I would be swept away with the wind.

The time to prepare is before Christ comes, and since you do not know when that will occur, the takeaway from today's reading is that you should always be ready. Are you ready? The only way to be ready is to be prepared. Today, invite the Lord to renew your heart and your desire for Him. Commit to adopting a daily Scripture reading (and memorization) regimen and invite the Lord to lead you through this process.

## Reflections on Christmas Eve

Scripture lesson for December 24th:

Luke 2:1-11 Now in those days a decree went out from Caesar Augustus, that a census be taken of all the inhabited earth. 2 This was the first census taken while Quirinius was governor of Syria. 3 And everyone was on his way to register for the census, each to his own city. 4 Joseph also went up from Galilee, from the city of Nazareth, to Judea, to the city of David which is called Bethlehem, because he was of the house and family of David, 5 in order to register along with Mary, who was engaged to him, and was with child. 6 While they were there, the days were completed for her to give birth. 7 And she gave birth to her firstborn son; and she wrapped Him in cloths, and laid Him in a manger, because there was no room for them in the inn. 8 In the same region there were some shepherds staying out in the fields and keeping watch over their flock by night. 9 And an angel of the Lord suddenly stood before them, and the glory of the Lord shone around them; and they were terribly frightened. 10 But the angel said to them, "Do not be afraid; for behold, I bring you good news of great joy which will be for all the people; 11 for today in the city of David there has been born for you a Savior, who is Christ the Lord.

~~~~~~~~~~~~~~~~~~~~~~~~~~~~~~~~

Tomorrow is Christmas, and it will be our last day together. I hope you have enjoyed this journey through the Christmas season and that it has reminded you of the things that are most important in life. I also hope that you have been able to see Christ in a new way or perhaps in a fresh way.

A few days ago you read about how you are the light of the world, and as we close our time together, I want to challenge you to think of yourself as a candle. Today in churches all across America, Christmas hymns will be sung. Messages anticipating the birth of Christ will be preached. And the traditional candle light service will begin while congregations sing *Silent Night*.

Imagine with me this picture in your church. The lights are turned off. The only light you see comes from the exit signs, the organist's lamp and the candles on the altar. Now imagine that the candles on the altar represent

Christ. He was sacrificed for you to present you blameless before God the Father just as the people of Israel made sacrifices on the altars of the Old Testament as an atonement for sin. The sacrifice of Christ on the altar gives off the light you see.

The minister or perhaps a few ushers light their candles from Christ. Now they go out into the dark world. They are sent, they have a mission, and they have a story to tell represented in the light they carry. The ushers light the candle held by the first person sitting in a row. And they go from row to row lighting the first person's candle. Now let's imagine that you are sitting next to this person. The minister instructs the people to not tip their lighted candles but instead for the person next to them (you) to tip the unlit candle into the flame.

So the person next to you extends his candle toward you, so that you can tip your candle into the flame. This is an invitation. Someone has just presented you with Christ. What are you going to do with Him? Will you accept? All too often the flame is passed on to the next person without thinking too deeply about the transaction that is occurring.

I hope that you will accept Him and welcome Him into your life. Unfortunately, it's not as easy as that. To light your candle, you have to extend *your own candle* and tip it into the flame of the person next to you. Yes, to truly accept Christ and the transformation He brings, action is required on your part. Christ stands at the door of your heart and knocks. He does not open the door but instead patiently waits for you to do the opening. Some have pointed out that the painting *Christ at Heart's Door* by Warner Sallman is significant because there is no handle or knob on the outside of the door. It could also be viewed as Christ patiently waiting for a response. Either way, action is required. What are you going to do with Christ?

When faced with Christ, you have to make a decision. There is no riding the fence here. Either you will accept Him or you will reject Him.

If you have not already done so, I would encourage you to let Him in today. Extend your candle and tip it into the flame and allow your heart to be on fire for Him. And having done so, your next decision must be to pass along the flame of salvation to your neighbor. Going back to the Christmas Eve candle light service, let's imagine that someone is sitting on the other side of you. Your candle is now lit. What are you going to do? Having accepted Christ and His salvation, *will you keep it to yourself or will you tell someone else about it*?

As the ushers move down the aisles and the people sitting closest to the aisle pass the flame of their candles along to the people next to them, the church begins to light up. I trust you made the decision to let your light shine brightly before all people of the world and that you have extended your flame to the person next to you. Now just about every candle in the church is light. First, look down the row you are in and see all the candles that have been lit. These lights were made possible because you accepted Christ and you made the decision to pass your flame along. If it were not for you, these people would not have light! Can you imagine what it would look like if your row was the *only row* in the whole church that did not have lit candles?

Yet, how is it that all too often people forget to extend the fire of their salvation to others? How will the world know about Christ unless we tell them, unless *you* tell them? And if you are not faithful in spreading the good news of the gospel message, will there be someone else? Are you prepared to take that chance?

Now look around our imaginary church. By now, everyone's candle has been lit. The church is full of light! The church is aglow with the fire of salvation. And if you continue the practice of accepting Christ and extending the fire of your salvation to others, the world will be aglow with the light of Christ! How wonderful would it be. And just think that it can all be made possible by your accepting Christ and extending the fire of your salvation into the world.

Won't you invite Him in today and allow Him to begin His transformation process in you?

## Christmas Day

Scripture lesson for December 25th:

Acts 1:-11 The first account I composed, Theophilus, about all that Jesus began to do and teach, 2 until the day when He was taken up to heaven, after He had by the Holy Spirit given orders to the apostles whom He had chosen. 3 To these He also presented Himself alive after His suffering, by many convincing proofs, appearing to them over a period of forty days and speaking of the things concerning the kingdom of God. 4 Gathering them together, He commanded them not to leave Jerusalem, but to wait for what the Father had promised, "Which," He said, "you heard of from Me; 5 for John baptized with water, but you will be baptized with the Holy Spirit not many days from now." 6 So when they had come together, they were asking Him, saying, "Lord, is it at this time You are restoring the kingdom to Israel?" 7 He said to them, "It is not for you to know times or epochs which the Father has fixed by His own authority; 8 but you will receive power when the Holy Spirit has come upon you; and you shall be My witnesses both in Jerusalem, and in all Judea and Samaria, and even to the remotest part of the earth." 9 And after He had said these things, He was lifted up while they were looking on, and a cloud received Him out of their sight. 10 And as they were gazing intently into the sky while He was going, behold, two men in white clothing stood beside them. 11 They also said, "Men of Galilee, why do you stand looking into the sky? This Jesus, who has been taken up from you into heaven, will come in just the same way as you have watched Him go into heaven."

~~~~~~~~~~~~~~~~~~~~~~~~~~~~~~

In recent years is has been said that Easter is the most important time of celebration for the follower of Christ because it is the time of Christ's resurrection. Christmas, they say, is no longer important because Christ's birth is in the past and, while it is all well and good to remember His entry into this world as a baby, your focus should be on His resurrection.

I agree that salvation is found in the resurrection of Christ and not in His birth. However, I disagree that Christmas should be relegated to minimal importance. We are still in a season of advent, a season of anticipation. The prophets of the Old Testament foretold of the triumphant coming of the

Messiah with salvation for all the world. But have today's followers of Christ forgotten that Christ will *come again* as the triumphant victor over all evil? Have they forgotten that followers of Christ shall meet Him in heaven one day? What do you mean the followers of Christ have nothing left to anticipate? Not only do you have something to anticipate, you have something to work toward!

In my childhood years, I never thought the excitement and allure of Christmas Day would ever end. Christmas is full of anticipation – how have others thought of me and how will others receive my gift? But as I have aged and now have children, Christmas does not hold the same excitement that it once did. Instead of racing to the tree on Christmas morning to see what was there for me, I now spend my time building up the anticipation in my children, and I spend my time preparing gifts for my children and find that once again it is hard to contain my excitement – not because I am receiving gifts but because I can't wait to see their reaction! Christmas is also exciting because it is a time of reunion with family – parents, siblings, nieces and nephews.

Although the allure I once had for Christmas has faded a little, I have so much to look forward to on Christmas Day. Still, it makes me wonder whether today's followers of Christ have allowed the wonder, excitement and allure of Christ to escape them. Often times, people who have just begun following Christ are full of passion and excitement for Christ, longing to see Christ one day, and to tell others about their new found joy. But as time wears on, this passion and excitement tend to fade, just like it does for us at Christmas-time.

But does that mean you have nothing left to be excited about? Nothing left to look forward to? Not at all! It is unfortunate that as passion and excitement fade, so does the desire to tell others about Christ. But you still have something wonderful to look forward to, and that is the second coming of Christ. You can also look forward to the reunion you will one day have with your loved ones who have gone on before you.

There is also another reason you have to look forward to the second coming of Christ, and that is your being redeemed and saved from evil. Christ paid the punishment for your sins and makes it possible for you to escape all punishment for your past mistakes and regrets. I am not much for tracts as a way of telling others about Christ, but one tract I saw was very unique. On the outside it said, "What you miss by being a Christian." And on the inside flap in big, bold letters was the word, "HELL."

I have just given you three reasons to still get excited about Christmas, and I encourage you to use the Christmas season as a reminder of what is yet to come – the advent of Christ's second coming. You have much to anticipate – and much to work toward. As we end our time together, I would encourage you to enter into a time of renewal in your relationship with Christ or to start your relationship with Christ for the first time. He wants you to become like Him and to be in communion with Him and to depend upon Him for everything you have need of. To begin your time of renewal, I encourage you to ask the Lord to search your heart, to know you and to see if there be any sin within you. With patience and diligent searching, you will find your answer, and the Lord will use your humility to shape you into the person He wants you to become.

If you are not following Christ but you have read this far, you shall be rewarded for seeking to learn more. It was once said that everyone has a God-shaped hole in their heart. I firmly believe this with every fiber of my being. Sadly, so many people go off seeking to fill this hole with things of the world which do not satisfy – narcotics, alcohol, promiscuity, divorce and remarriage. People even try to have this hole filled by their spouse or their children. Still others allow themselves to be validated by their peers, only to be disappointed, abused and taken advantage of. The only acceptance that matters and is worth having comes from Jesus Christ. His approval is sweet and His adoption of you into His family is joyful. Won't you let Him in today? Won't you accept the true gift of Christmas?

Recommended Follow-Up Reading During the Christmas Season

Church, Francis P., *Yes, Virginia, There Is A Santa Claus: The Classic Edition*, Running Press / 2001

Collins, Ace, *Stories Behind the Great Traditions of Christmas*, Zondervan / 2007

Id., *Stories Behind the Best-Loved Songs of Christmas*, Zondervan / 2007

Id., *More Stories Behind the Best-Loved Songs of Christmas*, Zondervan, 2007

Mackall, Dandi Daley, *The Legend of St. Nicholas: A Christmas Story of Giving*, Zondervan / 2007

Seuss, Dr., *How the Grinch Stole Christmas!*, Random House, Inc / 1957

Thompson, Lauren, *One Starry Night*, illustrated by Jonathan Bean, Margaret K. McElderry / 2011

About the Author

R. Joseph Ritter, Jr. is the son of a minister, born in Crisfield, Maryland, and raised in southeastern Pennsylvania. He is now married and has four children, and he has spent most of the last twenty-three years in Florida. Joe holds a degree in World Mission and Evangelism from Asbury Theological Seminary and has been a solo pastor and Director of Outreach in two churches. Joe is active in church leadership, including teaching Sunday school classes and Bible studies. He has also worked as a volunteer chaplain with Transport for Christ International and with his father was instrumental in forming Community Chaplains Association, a non-profit organization ministering to residents of assisted living and retirement facilities in Southeast Florida.

Made in the USA
Charleston, SC
14 November 2012